D1612235

A **Between Friends** collection by Sandra Bell-Lundy

Coffee, Tea, and Reality

Foreword by Lynn Johnston

Andrews McMeel
Publishing

Kansas City

ATTENTION: SCHOOLS AND BUSINESSES ——

For Donna, Marge, Lesley, Mary Ann, and Tracy

Foreword

Ever since *Between Friends* appeared in our paper, I've felt a kinship to Sandra Bell-Lundy and to the diverse characters she has created.

Sandra's tongue-in-cheek (that often gets bitten) style of writing is pure, personal, and funny. Her honesty draws you in. Her perspectives touch us all, making us want to join her heroines for a coffee—to unload and be one of them.

This is the woman-to-woman stuff said in grocery lines, at the office, or while commiserating over doughnuts at the kitchen table. This is the open door, the honest dialogue between the folks who have "been there."

It's a woman's world in which I feel welcome!

Lynn Johnston

8

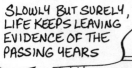

11

MOM? WHY DOESN'T MY FIRST MOMMY COME AND VISIT ME?

WELL, DANNY... SHE **WOULD** VISIT BUT SHE CAN'T GET HERE BECAUSE SHE'S UP IN HEAVEN

OH

COULDN'T WE THROW HER A ROPE?

MOMMY—WHEN DO PEOPLE DIE?

PEOPLE **ONLY** DIE WHEN THEY'RE **VERY** OLD

HOW OLD ARE **YOU**?

I'M NOT OLD AT ALL, DANNY, IN FACT, I'M VERY, VERY **YOUNG!**

I KNOW I DIDN'T ANSWER HIS QUESTION VERY HONESTLY, BUT THERE'S NO SENSE UPSETTING A PRESCHOOLER ABOUT THIS TYPE OF THING

I AGREE

HE DOESN'T NEED TO KNOW YOU'RE VERY, VERY **FORTY**

DANNY WAS SO YOUNG WHEN HIS MOTHER DIED, HE DOESN'T EVEN REMEMBER HER

WE KEEP HER PHOTO BY HIS BED... BUT SOMETIMES I STILL FEEL GUILTY ABOUT TREATING **HER** SON AS MY OWN

IT SEEMS SO UNFAIR TO HER THAT DANNY SEES **ME** AS HIS MOTHER... ¿SIGH¿... I WONDER WHAT **SHE'D** SAY ABOUT ALL THIS

THANK YOU

17

WHAT'S THE HARDEST PART OF BEING A NEW MOTHER, SUSAN?

ACCEPTING THAT MY FIGURE WILL NEVER BE THE SAME

??... BUT YOU ADOPTED... YOU'VE NEVER **BEEN** PREGNANT

I KNOW

THAT'S WHY IT'S HARD TO ACCEPT

DID YOU SEE THE PRETTY YOUNG WOMAN WE JUST PASSED ON THE PARK BENCH?

THE ONE WITH THE BIG BLUE EYES LIKE EMMA AND THE STRAWBERRY-BLOND HAIR LIKE EMMA?

YES- THAT'S THE ONE

WHAT ABOUT HER?

OH, I DON'T KNOW... I WAS JUST WONDERING...

-DOES SHE REMIND YOU OF ANYONE?

DO YOU SUPPOSE THAT YOUNG WOMAN COULD BE EMMA'S BIOLOGICAL MOTHER?

NYAH... COULDN'T BE

BUT HER HAIR IS EXACTLY EMMA'S COLOR!

PROBABLY CAME OUT OF A BOTTLE

...AND HER EYES ARE BIG AND BLUE LIKE EMMA'S

BLUE-BROWN... FIFTY-FIFTY SHOT

STILL- THERE'S A STRIKING RESEMBLANCE

IT'S A **PARK**, SUSAN... SHE'S PROBABLY JUST WATCHING HER KID PLAY ON THE SWINGS

YES... THE SAME THOUGHT OCCURRED TO ME

EMMA'S BIOLOGICAL MOTHER SURPRISED US IN THE PARK LAST WEEK... IT WAS QUITE UNSETTLING

SHE ASKED TO SEE EMMA AGAIN... I CAN HARDLY BELIEVE THIS!

NEITHER CAN **I**! WOW! YOU MET EMMA'S **REAL** MOTHER!

¿COUGH¿ ... I MEAN— WOW! YOU MET EMMA'S **BIOLOGICAL** MOTHER!

HOW DID EMMA'S BIRTH-MOTHER EVER FIND YOU?

HARV AND I DIDN'T SEAL THE ADOPTION RECORDS

WE WANTED TO KEEP AT LEAST ONE AVENUE OPEN TO PROVIDE AN OPPORTUNITY FOR THEM TO MEET

—JUST IN CASE THE DAY CAME WHEN THE BIRTH-MOTHER WAS READY AND EMMA WAS READY

THEN WHY ARE YOU SO UPSET?

BECAUSE **I'M** NOT READY!!

EMMA'S BIRTH-MOTHER ASKED TO MEET EMMA AGAIN

WHAT ARE YOU GOING TO DO?

I'M NOT SURE... THIS WHOLE SITUATION MAKES ME FEEL SO INSECURE

YOU SHOULDN'T FEEL THAT WAY, SUSAN

EMMA **LOVES** YOU! YOU CLOTHE HER, FEED HER, BATHE HER, READ TO HER, CUDDLE HER AND SOOTHE HER IN THE MIDDLE OF THE NIGHT... BELIEVE ME, **YOU'RE** HER **REAL** MOTHER

—AND YOU'VE GOT THE BAGS UNDER YOUR EYES TO PROVE IT!

WHY DOES EMMA'S BIRTH-MOTHER WANT TO MEET WITH YOU AGAIN?

SHE WANTS TO GIVE SOMETHING TO EMMA

MY HEAD SAYS "YES"... BECAUSE IT MAY BE A CONNECTION TO HER BIOLOGICAL ROOTS THAT SHE'LL WANT ONE DAY...

—BUT MY HEART SAYS "NO"...I DON'T WANT TO HAVE ANYTHING IN MY HOUSE THAT COMES FROM THIS WOMAN

...EXCEPT HER DAUGHTER

I'M SO GLAD YOU AGREED TO BRING EMMA TO THE PARK TODAY, SUSAN... I'M MOVING AWAY TO GO TO SCHOOL TOMORROW

I'VE BEEN WATCHING THE TWO OF YOU FOR A WHILE... AND I WANT TO TELL YOU I'M HAPPY YOU ADOPTED MY BABY

UH...YOU SAID YOU WANTED TO GIVE HER SOMETHING?

YES...IF YOU DON'T MIND, I'D LIKE TO GIVE HER MY PHOTO, MY FAVORITE DOLL...

...AND A RIDE ON THE SWINGS

I'M MOVING AWAY TOMORROW, SUSAN... AND IT'S NOT MY INTENTION TO INTERFERE IN YOUR LIFE...

—BUT SOMEDAY...WHEN EMMA IS OLDER AND ASKS ABOUT HER BIRTH-MOTHER...WOULD YOU GIVE HER MY PHOTO?

WELLL... I DON'T KNOW

...I'LL DO IT IF YOU'LL AGREE TO ONE CONDITION

WHAT IS IT?

TO TAKE THIS PHOTO OF EMMA AND ONCE IN A WHILE, LET ME SEND YOU MORE

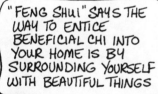

HAVING TWO YOUNG TEEN-AGERS TO SHOP FOR FORCES ME TO BE VERY CAREFUL WITH MY CLOTHING BUDGET

I'VE FOUND THE BEST WAY TO GET LONG-LASTING WEAR OUT OF MY WARDROBE IS TO STAY AWAY FROM FADS, WILD COLORS—

SPLUT

...AND GREASY FOODS

SOME CLOTHES JUST NEVER SEEM TO GO OUT OF STYLE

LIKE MY WEDDING DRESS... A SIMPLE, TIMELESS, TRADITIONAL GOWN THAT MY DAUGHTER WILL BE ABLE TO WEAR AND HER DAUGHTER AFTER THAT

WAS IT YOUR MOTHER'S?

ARE YOU KIDDING?

IT WAS MY **WEDDING DAY!** ... WHO WANTS TO WEAR A HAND-ME-DOWN DRESS?!

CREDIT CARD, DEBIT OR CHECK?

JUST CASH

—AIRMILES, COUPONS OR BONUS-POINTS CARD?

NO—NOTHING... JUST **CASH**

—HAVE YOU SIGNED UP FOR OUR PLATINUM CUSTOMER MEMBERSHIP PROGR—

NO! NO! JUST TAKE THE MONEY, OKAY? TAKE IT AND LET ME OUT OF HERE!

DIDN'T YOU GET YOUR GUM?

GUM? WAS THAT WHAT I WENT IN THERE FOR?

OH **NO**... NOT AGAIN!...

I CAN'T FIND MY LOCKER, ...I CAN'T REMEMBER MY COMBINATION...I DON'T KNOW WHERE MY BOOKS ARE AND I'VE LOST MY CLASS SCHEDULE...I **HATE** DREAMING I'M BACK IN HIGH SCHOOL!

I **HATE** THE FEELING OF BEING VULNERABLE, I **HATE** THE FEELING OF BEING CONFUSED AND I **HATE** THE FEELING OF BEING INSECURE

... I DO, HOWEVER, ENJOY THE FEELING OF BEING SIZE TEN...

MAYBE DREAMING I'M BACK IN HIGH SCHOOL IS ALLOWING MY SUB-CONSCIOUS TO DEAL WITH OLD INSECURITIES... LIKE MITCH BRADLEY...

THAT TURKEY ALWAYS INTIMIDATED ME WITH HIS WISECRACKS... BUT I'M NOT THE TONGUE-TIED TEENAGER I WAS TWENTY-SEVEN YEARS AGO

SO, GO AHEAD, TWERP... DO YOUR BEST- THERE'S NOTHING YOU CAN SAY TO MAKE ME BLUSH **NOW!**

HEY, LOSER- HOW COME YOU'RE IN YOUR BARE FEET?

GATOR

WHY THE HECK AM I DREAMING I'M IN MY HIGH-SCHOOL ENGLISH CLASS IN MY BARE FEET?!

WHY IS MY SUB-CONSCIOUS SUBJECTING ME TO THIS KIND OF HUMILIATION?

...ON THE OTHER HAND, WHY SHOULD I FEEL EMBARRASSED? THIS IS A **DREAM**

ALL I HAVE TO DO WHILE I WAIT TO WAKE UP IS PLAY IT COOL AND SLIDE MY BARE FEET UNDER MY—

HOUSECOAT?

36

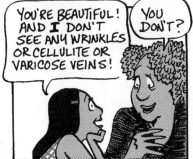

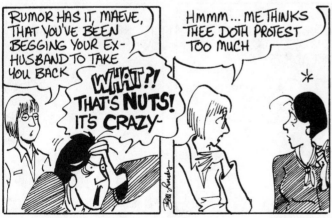

HM... I HAVEN'T NEEDED TO PLUCK MY EYEBROWS VERY OFTEN LATELY...

-THEY JUST DON'T SEEM TO BE GROWING IN AS MUCH AS THEY USED TO

WELL, **THERE'S** A PLUS I DIDN'T EXPECT WHEN THE OL' HORMONES STARTED SLOWING DOWN-

ONE LESS TEDIOUS, LITTLE GROOMING REGIMINE TO FOLLOW EVERY-

...MORNING

HOW A WOMAN WEARS HER HAIR IS A REFLECTION OF HER INDIVIDUAL PERSONA, HER OWN UNIQUE SENSE OF STYLE AND —

SUSAN! DO YOU REALIZE IT'S 8:15 AND IT'S YOUR TURN TO DROP EMMA AT THE SITTER'S ON YOUR WAY TO WORK?

BOOF

...HOW MUCH TIME SHE HAS IN THE MORNING

...¿SIGH?... I FINALLY GAVE IN, TINA... I CAVED...

HEY— IT HAPPENS TO THE BEST OF US

BUT ONCE YOU CROSS THAT LINE, IT'S A VERY SLIPPERY SLOPE

SLIPPERY, YES... BUT NOT NECESSARILY INSURMOUNTABLE

I JUST NEVER THOUGHT IT WOULD ACTUALLY COME TO THIS

BELIEVE ME, SUSAN ...IT COULD BE WORSE

WORSE? WHAT COULD BE WORSE THAN ELASTICIZED WAISTBANDS?

JUST WAIT UNTIL YOU STOOP TO 100% POLYESTER

IT RECENTLY DAWNED ON ME THAT I'VE CROSSED A WARDROBE GENERATION GAP

EVERYTHING I OWN IS "WASH AND WEAR"... I NOW CALL A QUARTER INCH A "HIGH" HEEL... AND LINEN OUTFITS ARE ANCIENT HISTORY

WHEN DID IT HAPPEN, SUSAN? WHEN DID "FUNCTIONAL" SURPASS "FASHIONABLE" AS THE REASON FOR BUYING OUR CLOTHES?

I'M NOT SURE, BUT I THINK IT WAS ABOUT THE TIME—

— "SLIMMING" SURPASSED "SEXY" AS THE REASON FOR BUYING BLACK

MRS. BARTELLI JUST CALLED... EMMA HAS BROKEN OUT WITH THE CHICKENPOX

I REMEMBER WHEN MY KIDS HAD THE CHICKENPOX... ¿SIGH¿ ... THE CONTINUAL OATMEAL BATHS, THE ITCHING, THE COMPLAINING, THE SLEEPLESS NIGHTS...

SOMEONE IS IN FOR A MISERABLE COUPLE OF DAYS

YOU POOR THING!

ONCE UPON A TIME, THERE WAS A YOUNG GIRL CALLED "CINDERELLA" BECAUSE SHE WOULD CLEAN THE CINDERS IN THE FIREPLACE

WOT'S "CINDERS"?

CINDERS ARE ASHES, HONEY

WOT'S "ASHES"?

WOOD TURNS INTO ASHES AFTER IT BURNS IN THE FIRE

WHERE'S ASCHES?

UH-WE DON'T HAVE ASHES ...THAT'S A GAS FLAME

WOT'S "GASCH"?

OH **LOOK!** "SLEEPING BEAUTY"! ...AND **HERE'S** "THE FROG PRINCE"...

CINDERELLA LIVED WITH HER WICKED STEP-MOTHER AND TWO STEPSISTERS

THEY WERE VERY MEAN TO HER AND TREATED HER AS A SERVANT

SEE THIS BIG HOUSE IN THE PICTURE, EMMA? CINDERELLA HAD TO DO **ALL** OF THE WASHING, SCRUBBING AND CLEAN-ING FOR IT

OOOOH...

- AND SHE DIDN'T **EVEN** HAVE A QUICKIE-CLEAN HOUSEKEEPING SERVICE TO HELP HER...

OOOOH...

MY ANNIVERSARY IS COMING UP, AND I'M LOOKING FOR SOMETHING ...UH... "SEXY"

I HAVE **JUST** THE THING! ...A SHEER, BLACK SILK NEGLIGEE WITH FAUX FUR TRIM

OOOOOOOOOOo! THAT'S **PERFECT**! IT'S **EXACTLY** WHAT I'VE BEEN LOOKING FOR!

...DOES IT COME IN FLANNEL WITH FIRM SUPPORT CUPS?

HAVE YOU NOTICED HOW YOUR FIGURE CHANGES THROUGH THE YEARS?

IT'S SO GRADUAL, OF COURSE, THAT YOU DON'T REALLY NOTICE THE DIFFERENCE AT FIRST...

-UNTIL SUDDENLY, ONE DAY, YOU LOOK IN THE MIRROR AND YOU ASK YOURSELF...

-WHEN THE HECK DID MY WAIST GET HIGHER?!

WITH CHRISTMAS COMING, WE REALLY SHOULD TRY TO TIGHTEN UP ON THE BUDGET

WHAT DO YOU SUGGEST?

WELL...WE COULD EAT LEFTOVERS MORE OFTEN

HM...OKAY

I'LL START ORDERING BIGGER TAKEOUT

53

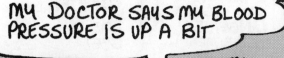
MY DOCTOR SAYS MY BLOOD PRESSURE IS UP A BIT

SHE SAYS I'M TOO STRESSED AND I NEED TO RELAX AND TAKE MORE DOWNTIME

HER SUGGESTION WAS TO SIGN UP FOR A YOGA CLASS THREE TIMES A WEEK, JOIN WATER FITNESS OR A LOW-IMPACT AEROBICS CLASS—

—AND GO FOR A TWENTY-MINUTE WALK AFTER DINNER EACH EVENING

THAT SOUNDS GOOD, ARE YOU GOING TO DO IT?

ARE YOU KIDDING?

Bell-Lundy

IF I HAD **THAT** MUCH TIME, I WOULDN'T BE STRESSED!

OH NO! THERE'S SIMON! I HOPE HE DIDN'T SEE ME...

THE LAST THING I WANT TO DO TODAY IS LISTEN TO MY EX-HUSBAND'S TESTOSTERONE-CHARGED ANECDOTES ABOUT HIS SOCIAL LIFE

-ESPECIALLY WHILE WE'RE SHOPPING IN THE MIDDLE OF A ...LINGERIE DEPARTMENT?...

...SIMON IS SHOPPING IN A LINGERIE DEPARTMENT?...

SIMON! LONG TIME NO SEE!

SO... WHAT WOULD YOU LIKE FOR CHRISTMAS, MAEVE?

ME?

WHAT DOES HE MEAN BY THAT? WHAT WOULD I LIKE FOR CHRISTMAS "IN GENERAL"... OR WHAT WOULD I LIKE FOR CHRISTMAS FROM "HIM"?

WE'VE BEEN DIVORCED FOR YEARS... WE DON'T EXCHANGE GIFTS! IS THIS SOME NEW POLITICALLY CORRECT THING? IS HE TRYING TO REKINDLE OUR RELATIONSHIP? HOW AM I SUPPOSED TO ANSWER THIS?!-

...MYSELF... I'D LIKE TO SKIP THE SNOW AND STICK WITH THIS UNSEASONABLY WARM WEATHER

I THINK MY EX-HUSBAND IS GOING TO BUY ME A GIFT FOR CHRISTMAS

WHY? WHAT DID HE SAY?

WELL-HE DIDN'T ACTUALLY SAY ANYTHING... BUT YOU KNOW HOW WE CAN READ THE SIGNS

-YOU MEAN WOMEN'S INTUITION?

YES... THAT...

-AND THIS LIST OF SIZES AND COLORS HE GAVE ME

SO - YOU THINK YOUR EX-HUSBAND IS BUYING YOU A CHRISTMAS GIFT, BUT YOU'RE NOT SURE...

WHAT'S THE BIG DILEMMA? JUST BUY HIM SOMETHING "IN CASE"..... EVEN IF HE DOESN'T GIVE YOU A GIFT, YOU CAN **STILL** GIVE **HIM** ONE...

DON'T YOU KNOW IT'S THE THOUGHT THAT COUNTS?

OF **COURSE** I KNOW IT'S THE THOUGHT THAT COUNTS

WHAT I **DON'T** KNOW IS HOW EXPENSIVE THE THOUGHT IS SUPPOSED TO BE

I'VE FINALLY DECIDED ON A CHRISTMAS GIFT FOR SIMON... "SOAP-ON-A-ROPE"

SEE HOW IT HANGS FROM THE SHOWER NOZZLE? IT'S THE PERFECT GIFT FOR AN EX-HUSBAND

I THINK IT HANGS **THIS** WAY, MAEVE

WHATEVER

HELLO, SIMON?... IT'S MAEVE... LISTEN - ABOUT YOU BUYING ME A GIFT FOR CHRISTMAS...

BUYING? YOU?...

- I THINK IT'S A WONDERFUL GESTURE FOR A DIVORCED MAN TO THINK OF HIS EX-WIFE LIKE THIS... BUT I CAN'T HELP FEELING THAT IT MIGHT LEAD TO COMPLICATED EXPECTATIONS IN THE FUTURE...

- SO I WOULD PREFER WE JUST CONTINUE TO MAIL EACH OTHER GREETING CARDS, OKAY?

UH... SURE, MAEVE... I UNDERSTAND COMPLETELY

SHE EXPECTS ME TO BUY HER A GIFT

IS IT? ... IS IT? ... IT IS!

GRANT GOLDOB! FROM MY OLD HIGH-SCHOOL DAYS AT GRANTHAM!

SUSAN DANIELS! FROM MY OLD HIGH-SCHOOL DAYS AT GRANTHAM!

DOES HE RECOGNIZE ME? NYAH, PROBABLY NOT...

DOES SHE RECOGNIZE ME? NYAH, PROBABLY NOT...

OTHERWISE HE/SHE WOULD HAVE SAID "HELLO"

IT'S NICE TO SEE YOU AGAIN, SUSAN! SAY— DID YOU GET YOUR INVITATION TO OUR HIGH-SCHOOL REUNION?

REUNION?... UH... NO... NOT YET...

NOT **YET**?! **I** GOT **MINE** MONTHS AGO...

MONTHS AGO?.... WELL... MINE MUST BE.. I MEAN.. IT COULD HAVE... ER...

—SO DID LINDA MORRICH, JIM PEMLER, DIANE BATCOM, BOB CHALMERS, TINA DUNBAR—

...SIGH... OLD HIGH-SCHOOL INSECURITIES NEVER DIE....

—THEY JUST CHEW YOU UP AND SPIT YOU OUT EVERY CLASS REUNION

...ARE YOU **SURE** YOU **WENT** TO GRANTHAM?—

I SAW GRANT GOLDOB IN THE GROCERY STORE TODAY

GRANT GOLDOB FROM HIGH SCHOOL? DID YOU SAY HELLO?

OH, YES! WE MUST HAVE CHATTED FOR TWENTY MINUTES OR MORE! HE TOLD ME ABOUT HIS LIFE, AND I TOLD HIM ABOUT MINE

YOU KNOW... IT WAS KIND OF WEIRD STANDING THERE IN THE PRODUCE AISLE WITH HIM... LAUGHING AND JOKING LIKE THAT

BECAUSE SO MANY YEARS HAVE PASSED?

BECAUSE WE NEVER SAID A **WORD** IN SCHOOL

GEE, IT'LL BE GREAT TO GO TO OUR HIGH-SCHOOL REUNION AND SEE GOOD OL' GRANTHAM AGAIN

"SEE" GRANTHAM?

DIDN'T YOU **HEAR?** OUR SCHOOL WAS SOLD **AGES** AGO- IT'S BEEN CONVERTED TO A PHARMACEUTICAL RESEARCH FACILITY... WE'RE NOT EVEN ALLOWED **IN** THE PLACE!

THEY'RE USING ANOTHER SCHOOL AS A REPLACEMENT

YOU MEAN WE'RE SUPPOSED TO RELIVE OUR MEMORIES IN ANOTHER SCHOOL?!

WHAT THE HECK DO YOU CALL **THAT**?

VIRTUAL NOSTALGIA

MY OLD HIGH SCHOOL IS HAVING A REUNION IN THE SPRING

AGAIN? WHY?

"WHY"? TO REMINISCE! TO CATCH UP! TO SEE OLD FRIENDS!

BUT THEY JUST HAD A REUNION A LITTLE WHILE AGO

THAT WAS **TEN YEARS** AGO! LOTS CAN HAPPEN IN TEN YEARS, YOU KNOW!

...LOTS AND **LOTS**...

AT OUR LAST HIGH-SCHOOL REUNION, I WAS INTIMIDATED TO COMPARE NOTES WITH OUR OLD CLASSMATES

I WAS AFRAID I WOULDN'T BE AS SUCCESSFUL AS EVERYONE ELSE, AND THEY'D THINK I HADN'T ACCOMPLISHED VERY MUCH

BUT THAT WAS **THEN** AND THIS IS **NOW**... THIS REUNION IS GOING TO BE DIFFERENT!

BECAUSE YOU'VE COME TO TERMS WITH YOUR OWN SELF-WORTH?

THAT AND I'M GOING TO LIE

JANET IS TAKING AN EVENING COURSE AT THE UNIVERSITY, GRACE IS ORGANIZING A WEEKLY BOOK CLUB MEETING...

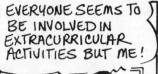

EVERYONE SEEMS TO BE INVOLVED IN EXTRACURRICULAR ACTIVITIES BUT ME!

I CAN'T EVEN MANAGE TO GET TO THE GYM ONCE A WEEK! I JUST DON'T HAVE THE TIME!

WHAT'S WRONG WITH "NOW"?

I JUST DON'T HAVE THE ENERGY

I WORK ALL DAY, COME HOME, MAKE DINNER, CLEAN UP AND PLOP DOWN ON THE COUCH

HOW CAN I DEVELOP ANY SPIRITUAL GROWTH OR FIND ANY PERSONAL ENRICHMENT BY JUST SITTING AT HOME?

HOW CAN I NOT?

MY BEAUTIFUL, CLEVER, LITTLE DAUGHTER...

SO MANY OPPORTUNITIES FOR YOU IN LIFE... I WONDER WHO YOU'LL BE?... GLORIA STEINEM?... CELINE DION?... HILLARY CLINTON?

I BE "EMMA"

MY BEAUTIFUL, CLEVER, LITTLE DAUGHTER

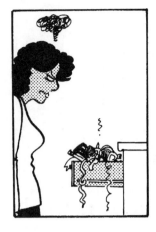

... PERSONALLY, I DON'T BELIEVE IN THE TERM "GENERATION GAP"...

−THAT PHRASE IS NOTHING MORE THAN AN EXCUSE TO EXPLAIN AWAY A LACK OF APPRECIATION FOR DIFFERENT VALUES ...IN OTHER WORDS, "INTOLERANCE"

−AND INTOLERANCE BREEDS FRUSTRATION, ANGER AND FINALLY... "CONFRONTATION"

IT ALL BOILS DOWN TO ONE THING, REALLY− RESPECT FOR THE DIFFERENCES AND PREFERENCES OF EVERYONE... NOT JUST A SELECT FEW!

DO YOU UNDERSTAND WHAT I'M SAYING?

YES, **I** DO... BUT LIKE I TOLD YOU BEFORE

MY MANAGER JUST WON'T **LET** US SUBSTITUTE COFFEE FOR SOFT DRINKS IN A COMBO MEAL...

SPECIAL
LOW FAT
COMBO NO.4
COMBO NO.5

LISTEN TO THIS — YALE UNIVERSITY DID A STUDY ON THE PSYCHOLOGY OF BAD HAIR DAYS...

THEY DETERMINED BAD HAIR MADE PEOPLE FEEL LESS SMART, LESS CAPABLE AND LESS SOCIABLE — **AND,** CONTRARY TO POPULAR BELIEF—

—THEY FOUND IT HAD A STRONGER EFFECT ON MEN THAN WOMEN! ...WELL, WHAT DOES **THAT** TELL YOU?

THAT I'M SENDING MY KIDS TO HARVARD

HAVE YOU EXPERIENCED ANY MENOPAUSAL SYMPTOMS YET?

NOT REALLY—

...JUST THE OCCASIONAL HOT FLASH

HARV— YOU LOOK TIRED ...WHY DON'T YOU AND EMMA GO FOR A WALK WHILE I MAKE DINNER?

YOU TWO COULD USE SOME FRESH AIR AND THE EXERCISE WILL HELP YOU BOTH GET A GOOD NIGHT'S SLEEP

...MOTHERHOOD... FOR SOME REASON IT MAKES YOU WANT TO NURTURE EVERYONE...

...BUT YOURSELF...

I'VE TRIED **EVERYTHING** TO GET EMMA TO STOP SUCKING HER THUMB... BAD-TASTING NAIL POLISH... TAPE... BRIBERY... **NOTHING** WORKS!

IF SHE'S BUSY, SHE FORGETS ABOUT IT, BUT AS SOON AS SHE RELAXES — **BAM!** — IT GOES RIGHT IN HER MOUTH!

SHEESH... KIDS! ONCE THEY GET HOLD OF A HABIT, IT'S LIKE A CRUTCH THEY JUST CAN'T LET GO OF!

REFILL?

CAN YOU LEAVE THE POT?

I'VE FOUND THAT THE QUALITIES I APPRECIATE MOST IN A MAN HAVE CHANGED OVER THE YEARS

I USED TO THINK APPEARANCE WAS IMPORTANT... THEN I THOUGHT FINANCIAL SUCCESS WAS ATTRACTIVE...

— BUT NOW I REALIZE THAT TO EXPERIENCE TRUE JOY IN A RELATIONSHIP, IT'S VITAL FOR A MAN TO HAVE AN APPRECIATION FOR HUMOR

... MINE

... OUR OLD HIGH SCHOOL WAS SOLD AND TRANSFORMED INTO A PHARMACEUTICAL RESEARCH FACILITY...

— THE LITTLE PAR 3 GOLF COURSE WE WORKED AT AFTER SCHOOL WAS BULL-DOZED TO THE GROUND AND IS NOW A SHOPPING MALL...

THE TANGIBLE SYMBOLS OF MY YOUTH... REDUCED TO MEMORIES ... ¿SIGH? ... DOESN'T **ANYTHING** IN THIS LIFE LAST FOREVER?

JUST THIGH CELLULITE, MAEVE... JUST THIGH CELLULITE...

YOU KNOW—THIS PREOCCUPATION WITH "AGE" IS RIDICULOUS...

YOU CAN'T MEASURE A PERSON'S DEVELOPMENT BY HOW MANY BIRTHDAYS THEY'VE CELEBRATED

THE COMPLEXITIES OF MATURITY AND GROWTH ARE DEFINED BY MUCH MORE SUBTLE INDICATORS

LIKE WHAT?

NECK WADDLE, FOR ONE

YOU KNOW—WE'RE **LUCKY** TO BE FORTY IN THIS DAY AND AGE... LOOK AT THE ROLE MODELS WE HAVE...

SUSAN SARANDON, MICHELLE PFEIFFER, RENE RUSSO...TALK ABOUT YOUR **SEXY** OLDER WOMEN!

NO ONE WOULD CALL **THESE** WOMEN "OVER-THE-HILL"...THEY ARE **HOT!**

DO YOU THINK **WE'LL** BE HOT A DECADE FROM NOW?

WE WILL IF ESTROGEN HAS ANYTHING TO DO WITH IT

YOU KNOW, HARV... THE OLDER I GET, THE MORE I COME TO REALIZE THE TRULY IMPORTANT THINGS IN LIFE

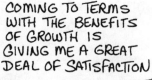

COMING TO TERMS WITH THE BENEFITS OF GROWTH IS GIVING ME A GREAT DEAL OF SATISFACTION

YEP—THERE IS DEFINITELY AN ALLURE TO MATURITY

I'LL SAY

COMPOUNDED INTEREST

...It suddenly dawned on the princess just how badly she had treated the frog...

Forgetting her disgust at his ugly appearance, she leaned over and kissed him tenderly

To her utter amazement, the repulsive little frog vanished

POOF

Her kind heart had changed him into a handsome prince

UH-HUH... I SEE...

WELL, I GUESS THAT ANSWERS MY QUESTION, "WHAT DOES HE LOOK LIKE?"

OH! AND DID I MENTION HIS SENSE OF HUMOR?-

BellLundy

AFTER WATCHING THE ERIN BROCKOVICH VIDEO...

WOW... **HOW** DID SHE EVER SURVIVE AS A SINGLE MOTHER WITH THREE KIDS?

HOW DID SHE EVER FIND THE TENACITY TO PURSUE INVESTIGATING THE WATER CONTAMINATION?

HOW DID SHE ENDURE WEARING THOSE PUSH-UP BRAS DAY AFTER **DAY**? —

LEAVING THE KIDS AT DAY CARE AND MEETING FOR LUNCH WAS A **WONDERFUL** IDEA, SUSAN!

WE HAVEN'T DONE ANYTHING LIKE THIS FOR **AGES**!

I KNOW... I FEEL SUCH A SENSE OF WILD, UNINHIBITED **ABANDON**!

WE'RE FREE-**FREE FREE!**

... FOR THE NEXT... TWO HOURS AND FORTY-FIVE MINUTES

I MAY HAVE TO CUT THAT A BIT SHORT...

—NOT THAT I DON'T LOVE SPENDING TIME WITH MY DAUGHTER... BUT LUNCH WITH NO KIDS IS **WONDERFUL**!

YES... THE DECORUM AND THE PEACE ARE JUST **HEAVENLY**! ... NOT THAT I DON'T ADORE BEING WITH MY SON

SIGH

YOU KNOW YOU'RE A MOTHER WHEN YOU FEEL THE NEED TO CLARIFY YOUR FREE TIME

MONDAY	TUESDAY	WEDNESDAY

ENOUGH IS ENOUGH! ... I'M GOING TO START WORKING OUT AT THE GYM **EVERY** DAY!

I SUPPOSE IT WOULDN'T HURT TO SKIP THE TREADMILL TODAY ... AFTERALL I **WAS** HERE YESTERDAY ...

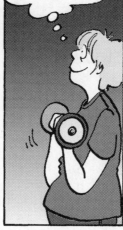

THREE DAYS IN A ROW! I'D SAY I DESERVE A DONUT ON THE WAY HOME ...

THURSDAY	FRIDAY	SATURDAY

... MAYBE I'LL STOP FOR THE DONUT **FIRST** ...

WHAT THE HECK ... THE GYM CLOSED FIFTEEN MINUTES AGO **ANYWAY** ...

WHAT? NOT WORKING OUT TODAY?

ENOUGH IS ENOUGH, HARV ... IT'S SATURDAY FOR PETE'S SAKE

WHAT A CRUSHER DAY! I CAN'T WAIT TO GET HOME AND HAVE MY DAILY LITTLE "PICK-ME-UP"

"DAILY"? BETTER BE CAREFUL, SUSAN–THOSE LITTLE "PICK-ME-UPS" CAN BECOME ADDICTIVE, YOU KNOW

YES...

–I KNOW

MAEVE! YOU'VE CHANGED YOUR HAIR!

YES

I WENT TO THAT NEW SALON DOWNTOWN. IT WAS EXPENSIVE BUT IT WAS WORTH IT TO GET A PROFESSIONAL STYLING

THEY CALL THIS "THE TOUSLED LOOK"...WHAT DO YOU THINK?

THAT I COULD HAVE SAVED YOU SOME MONEY

WE'VE CHANGED A LOT IN THE LAST FEW YEARS

WE HAVE?

WE'VE REACHED THE STAGE WHERE WE'RE CONFIDENT WITH OUR MATURITY ... WE BUY SOPHISTICATED FASHIONS, WE GET SEXY HAIR-STYLES AND WE WEAR DRAMATIC COLORS

COME TO THINK OF IT, YOU **DO** HAVE A POINT... AFTER ALL–

–THERE **WAS** A TIME I WOULDN'T BE CAUGHT **DEAD** IN GRAPE

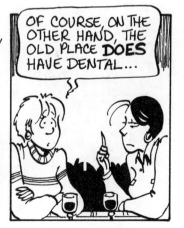

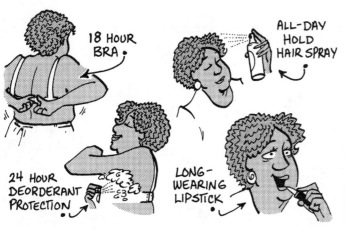

18 HOUR BRA

24 HOUR DEODERANT PROTECTION

ALL-DAY HOLD HAIR SPRAY

LONG-WEARING LIPSTICK

THERE

NOW ALL I NEED IS A 32 HOUR DAY AND I'M SET

Bill Lundy

IT'S A STUPID HABIT

I SUPPOSE SO...

—BUT WHEN YOU LIVE IN A SOCIETY, IT'S DIFFICULT NOT TO BE INFLUENCED BY ITS CULTURAL MORES

—WHICH IS WHY, EVEN THOUGH IT DOESN'T MAKE SENSE ON A PURELY RATIONAL LEVEL, I HAVE TO ADMIT—

—THAT I STILL FEEL MORE ATTRACTIVE WHEN I SHAVE MY LEGS

Bill Lundy

OUCH!! @*#%!!
WHY AM I DOING THIS TO MYSELF?! THIS IS **NUTS!**

WHO STARTED THIS STUPID CUSTOM OF WOMEN SHAVING THEIR LEGS ANYWAY?! I MEAN—*REALLY!*

DOES OUR SOCIETY **HONESTLY** BELIEVE THAT LESS HAIR MEANS MORE HAPPINESS?!

NOT IN ALL CASES

Bill Lundy

SEEMS LIKE EVERY TIME I LOOK IN THE MIRROR, I FIND A NEW WRINKLE OR A FEW MORE GREY HAIRS

≷SIGH≷... I GUESS OUR "SEXY" DAYS ARE OVER

OVER? SAYS WHO?!

I CAN'T STAND THIS NAVEL-GAZING ATTITUDE THAT SEX APPEAL IS RESERVED FOR TWENTY-SOMETHINGS!

WHY DO WE **ALWAYS** HAVE TO LABEL AND CATEGORIZE A PERSON ACCORDING TO THEIR AGE?!

I MEAN... LOOK AT PAUL NEWMAN...

- WHO WOULD SAY THAT OLD GEEZER ISN'T CUTE?

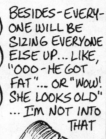

≶SIGH≶ ...I WISH I COULD FIND JANICE TARTLE... SHE'S ONE PERSON I **REALLY** WANT TO SEE

JANICE TARTLE?!

BOY- DID I GET THE SCOOP ON **HER**! SHE'S THE ADMINISTRATOR FOR A MAJOR WOMEN'S HOSPITAL! TALK ABOUT SUCCESS! POWER!... PRESTIGE!... SIX-FIGURE INCOME!... SHE'S GOT IT **ALL**!

THEN... SHE'S **HERE**?!

NO...SHE COULDN'T MAKE IT

THANK GOODNESS... SHE'S ONE PERSON I **REALLY** DON'T WANT TO SEE...

DAVE TRUSCOTT! REMEMBER ME?!

UH...SORRY, I'M AFRAID I DON'T

IT'S SUSAN! SUSAN DANIELS! WE WENT THROUGH FOUR YEARS OF HIGH SCHOOL TOGETHER!

WE **DID**? GEE... SORRY, BUT I DON'T SEEM TO REMEMBER

OH, GIVE ME A BREAK! HOW CAN ANYONE FORGET A PERSON WHO WAS IN THE SAME SCHOOL WITH THEM FOR FOUR YEARS?! IT'S RIDICULOUS!... IT'S SELF-ABSORBED! ...IT'S—

SUSAN! REMEMBER ME?! FRANK MEYERS!

FRANK **WHO**?...

LOOK AT THE TURNOUT FOR THIS REUNION! HIGH-SCHOOL GRADS FROM THE FIFTIES TO THE NINETIES!

UH-HUH... BIG CROWD

IT MUST HAVE TAKEN THE REUNION COMMITTEE A **LOT** OF WORK TO PULL THIS OFF

I HEARD HUNDREDS OF HOURS

WE SHOULD GO AND THANK THEM FOR ALL THEIR EFFORTS

THEY'RE OVER THERE... SIGNING UP VOLUNTEERS FOR THE **NEXT** REUNION

OF COURSE, WE **COULD** JUST MAIL THEM A CARD...

—OR THERE'S FAX... FAX IS GOOD...

108

SHRIEEEEEEEEEEEK

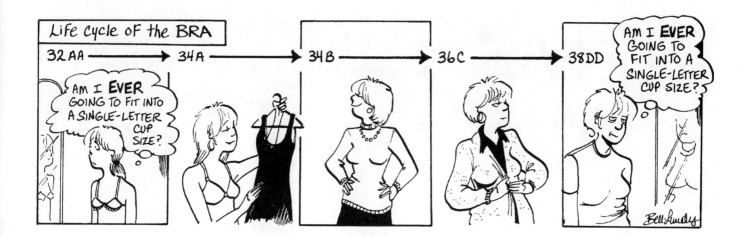

HEY—LOOK AT THIS... "ENHANCE YOUR BUST-LINE WITH THE NEW WATER BRA"

INSTEAD OF CUSHION PADDING, THE CUPS ARE FILLED WITH LIQUID FOR A MORE NATURAL CLEAVAGE

BREAST ENLARGEMENT WITH LIQUID PADDING... HM... I WONDER WHO DREAMT UP THAT IDEA

PROBABLY A MAN

WHO ELSE WOULD TRY TO SELL WATER RETENTION TO A WOMAN?

BRASSIERES

≥SIGH≤

YOU KNOW YOU'RE GETTING OLDER WHEN YOU CAN'T FIND A BRA THAT COSTS LESS THAN YOUR JEANS

WILL THAT BE DEBIT, CREDIT OR OUR CONVENIENT LAY-A-WAY PLAN?

TRUST ME

WELL-L-L ...OKAY, I'LL GIVE IT A SHOT

KISS

POOF

I KNEW IT! I KNEW IT!

WHAT KIND OF GAG IS **THIS**?! YOU **SAID** YOU WERE A HANDSOME PRINCE!

YOU DON'T THINK I'M HANDSOME?

OH, NOW **THIS** IS JUST WONDERFUL... I DUCK OUT TO PICK UP SOME FAST FOOD AFTER PAINTING MY KITCHEN ALL DAY—

—AND I RUN INTO LORNA SHELBORNE... THE MOST WELL-DRESSED AND BIGGEST **SNOB** I EVER WENT TO HIGH SCHOOL WITH!

SHE ALWAYS MADE ME FEEL SO INSECURE BECAUSE I HAD HOME-SEWN CLOTHES AND SHE ALWAYS HAD EXPENSIVE STORE-BOUGHT

SUSAN—**SUSAN**! COMPOSE YOURSELF! THIS IS TWENTY-FIVE YEARS LATER! YOU'VE MATURED! YOU'VE DEVELOPED POISE AND GRACE!

—AND THOSE ARE THE QUALITIES THAT WILL SHINE THROUGH A MEASLY FEW PAINT SPLATTERS

SUSAN! SUSAN DANIELS! IT'S BEEN **YEARS**! HOW **ARE** YOU?!

USUALLY A **LOT** BETTER DRESSED THAN THIS!!

120

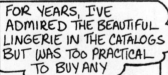